Mel Bay Presents

20 Celtic Fingerstyle Uke Tunes

by Rob MacKillop

CD Contents

1 The Bank of Ireland	11 John McHugh's Jig
2 The Lilting Banshee	12 The Mug of Brown Ale
3 The Blarney Pilgrim	13 The Star of Munster
4 Da Foula Reel	14 Jig: Queen Margaret University
5 Drowsy Maggie	15 The Connaught Man's Rambles
6 Fairy Dance	16 Sleepy Maggie
7 Flowers of the Forest	17 The Congress
8 The Glass of Beer	18 Tripping Upstairs
9 The Humours of Glendart	19 The Humours of Tulla
10 Kesh Jig	20 The Wind that Shakes the Barley

Visit www.FingerstyleUke.com for more publications

1 2 3 4 5 6 7 8 9 0

Visit us on the Web at www.melbay.com — E-mail us at email@melbay.com

The Celtic Uke

Rob MacKillop

Contents

Introduction

I've brought together twenty of my favorite Scots and Irish tunes in arrangements for ukulele, an instrument for which–I hope you will agree–this music is particularly suited.

In making the arrangements I had to decide whether or not to retain the original keys. Traditional session tunes rarely appear in different keys, but this sometimes causes a problem when they are transferred to the unique tuning of the high G or high A uke. I decided to arrange the pieces as best suited the instrument. As uke players, we have a choice of playing from tab on different-sized instruments such as baritone, tenor, concert and soprano, each of which could be tuned to a different pitch. Plus there is the possible use of the capo. So it should be possible for those who are keen to play in sessions to find the right key. This seems a preferable approach to making awkward and unnecessarily difficult arrangements of music which should be free flowing. I think these arrangements fit the instrument beautifully, and I hope you enjoy working them into your repertoire.

Please visit MelBay.com for more of my publications.

Rob MacKillop
Edinburgh, 2010

The Bank of Ireland
[Original in D]

Traditional
arr. Rob MacKillop ©

The Lilting Banshee
[Original in G]

Traditional
arr. Rob MacKillop ©

The Blarney Pilgrim
[Original in G]

Traditional
arr. Rob MacKillop

Da Foula Reel

Traditional
arr. Rob MacKillop ©

Drowsy Maggie

Traditional
arr. Rob MacKillop ©

Fairy Dance

Traditional
arr. Rob MacKillop ©

Flowers of the Forest

Traditional
arr. Rob MacKillop ©

The Glass of Beer
[Original in Bm]

Traditional
arr. Rob MacKillop ©

The Humours of Glendart
[Original in D]

Traditional
arr. Rob MacKillop ©

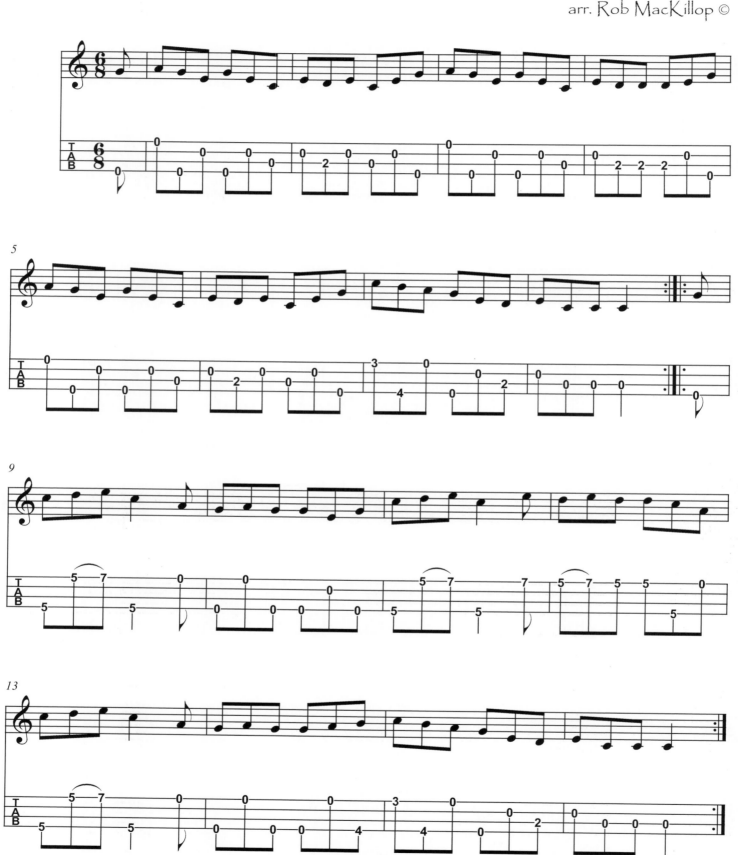

Kesh Jig

Traditional
arr. Rob MacKillop ©

John McHugh's Jig

Traditional
arr. Rob MacKillop ©

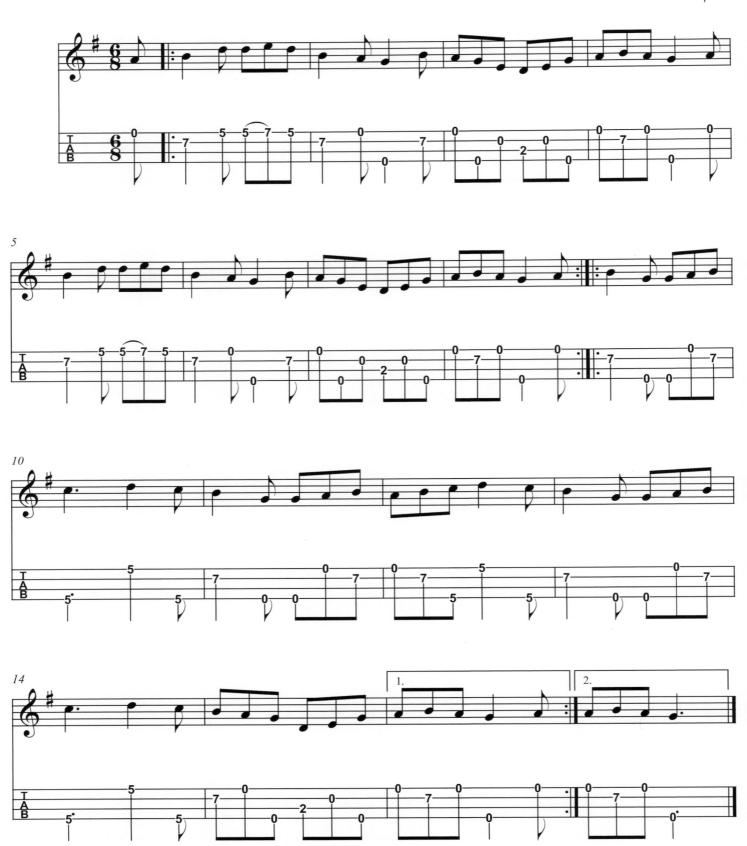

The Mug of Brown Ale

[Original in Am]

Traditional
arr. Rob MacKillop ©

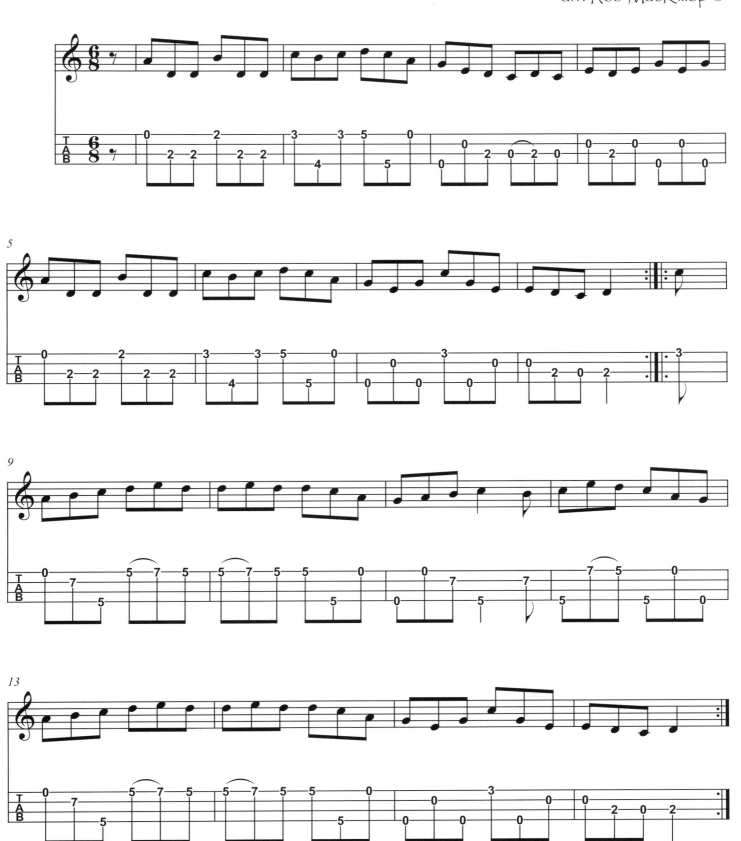

The Star of Munster
[Original in Am]

Traditional
arr. Rob MacKillop ©

This page has been left blank
to avoid awkward page turns.

Jig: Queen Margaret University

Written in celebration of QMCU becoming QMU, with a nod to Tom Anderson, who wrote 'March: Queen Margaret College'. Rob MacKillop, 5/2/07

Form: AABBAACCAA

Rob MacKillop ©

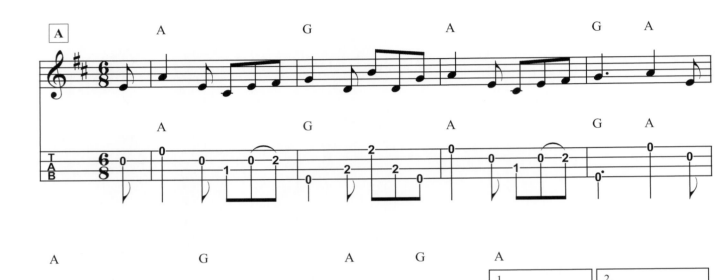

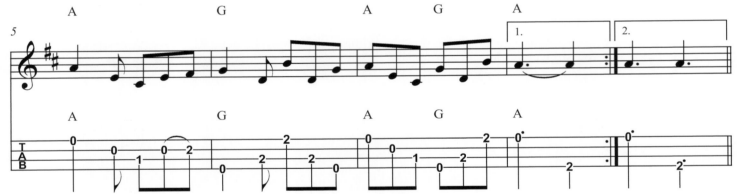

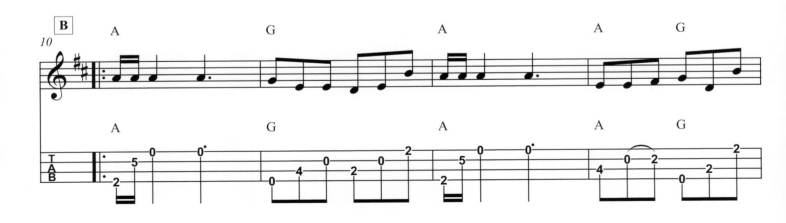

The Connaught Man's Rambles

[Original in D]

Traditional
arr. Rob MacKillop ©

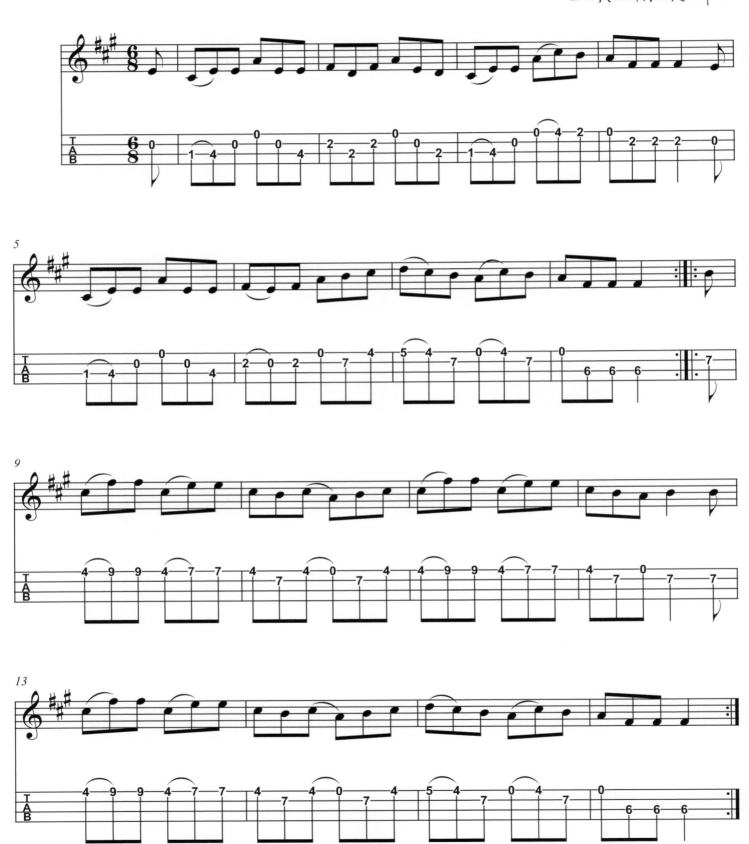

Sleepy Maggie

Traditional
arr. Rob MacKillop ©

The Congress
[Originally in Am]

Traditional
arr. Rob MacKillop ©

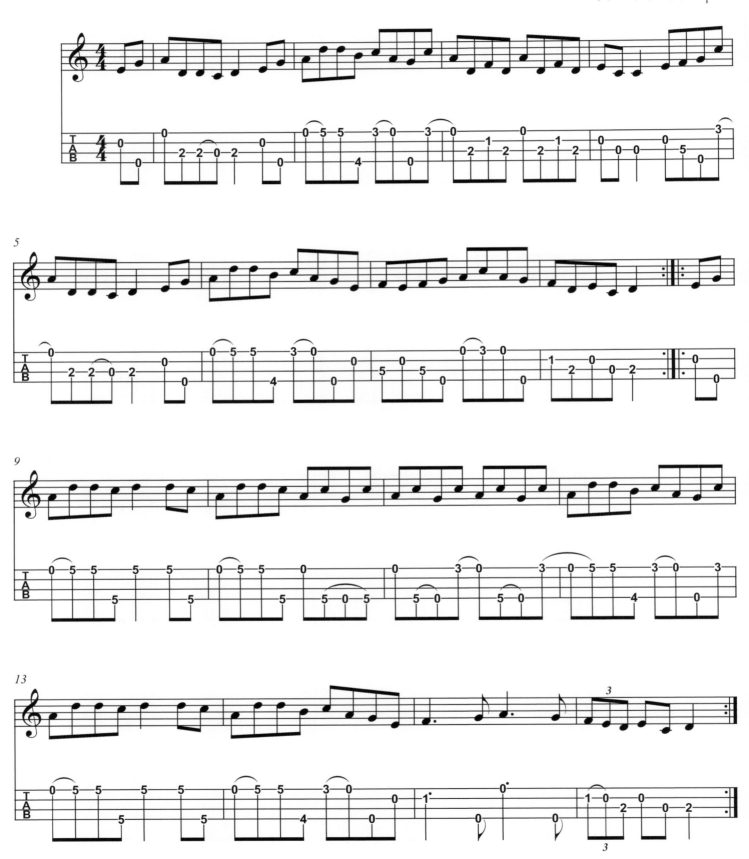

Tripping Upstairs
[Original in D]

Traditional
arr. Rob MacKillop ©

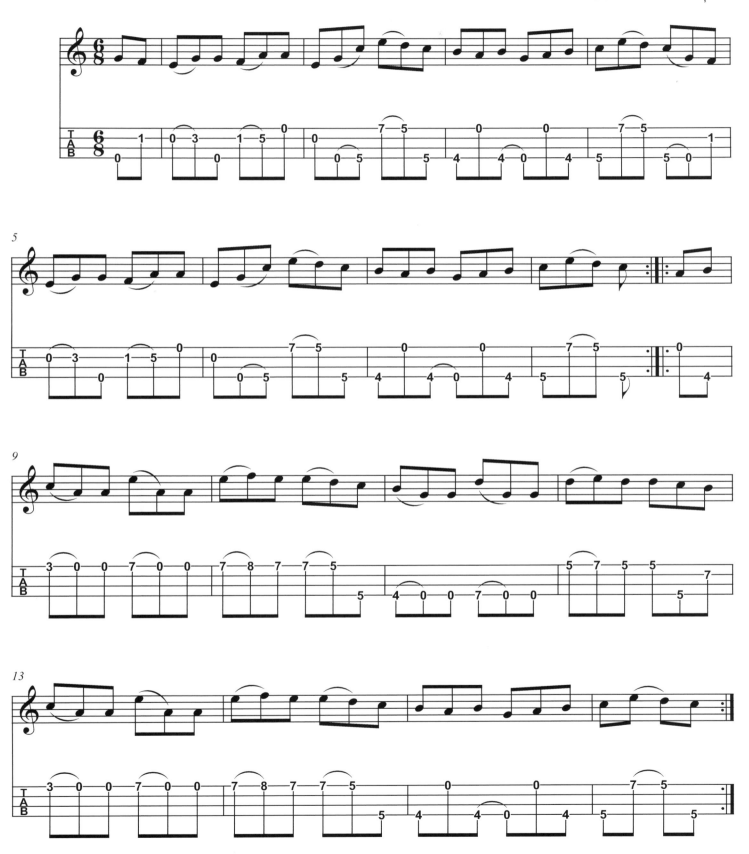

The Humours of Tulla
[Original in D]

Traditional
arr. Rob MacKillop ©

The Wind that Shakes the Barley
[Originally in D]

Traditional
arr. Rob MacKillop ©

Rob MacKillop

Rob MacKillop is an Early Music specialist with recordings, performances and academic essays in historical lutes, ukuleles and guitars. He has brought the same practices to the early banjo, seeking out early instruments, repertoire and techniques.

"One of Scotland's finest musicians" *Celtic World*

"A top-drawer player" *Early Music Today*

"A true champion of Scottish music" *The Herald*

"A player of real quality, with warmth of personality and communication skills to match...one of Scotland's top professionals" *Classical Guitar*

"MacKillop displays dazzling virtuosity...the playing is exceptionally musical" *Sounding Strings*

"A leading traditional talent who is single-handedly responsible for unearthing some of the nation's finest music" *The Scotsman*

Rob MacKillop has recorded eight CDs of historical music, three of which reached the Number One position in the Scottish Classical Music Chart. In 2001 he was awarded a Churchill Fellowship for his research into medieval Scottish music, which led him to studying with Sufi musicians in Istanbul and Morocco. He broadcasted an entire solo concert on BBC Radio 3 from John Smith's Square, London.

He has presented academic papers at conferences in Portugal and Germany, and has been published many times. Rob has been active in both historical and contemporary music.

Three of Scotland's leading contemporary composers have written works for him, and he also composes new works himself. In 2004 he was Composer in Residence for Morgan Academy in Dundee, and in 2001 was Musician in Residence for Madras College in St Andrews. He created and Directed the Dundee Summer Music Festival.

He worked as a Reader of schools literature for Oxford University Press, and as a reviewer for *Music Teacher*. He has also been Lecturer in Scottish Musical History at Aberdeen University, Dundee University, and at the Royal Scottish Academy of Music and Drama.

He is presently Musician In Residence to Queen Margaret University in Edinburgh, and a regular article writer for BMG magazine.

Rob plays banjo, guitar and ukulele with gut strings, plucking the strings with the flesh of his fingers, not the nails. This produces a warm and intimate sound, reminiscent of the old lute players.

Rob MacKillop's main websites are www.RobMacKillop.net and www.ClassicBanjoRM.com

Checkout www.MelBay.com for more editions by Rob MacKillop